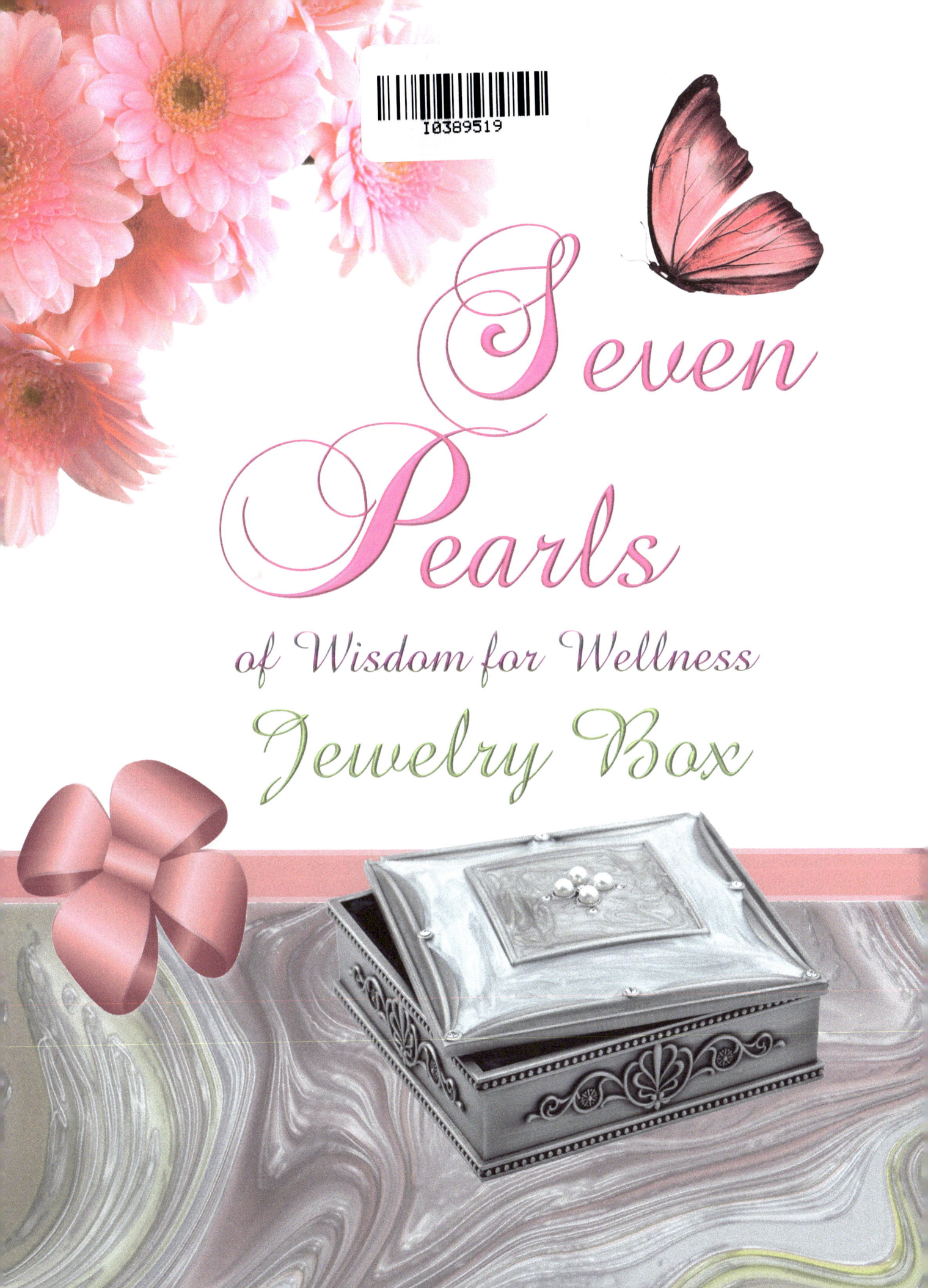

Seven Pearls
of Wisdom for Wellness
Jewelry Box

Seven Pearls of Wisdom for Wellness
Jewelry Box

This Lifebook is not intended as a substitute for the medical advice of physicians or other health professionals. The reader should regularly consult a physician in matters relating to his/her health and particularly with respect to any symptoms that may require diagnosis or medical attention.

© by Sagesse Life Promotions
To request permissions
info@sagesselife.com
First Edition November 30, 2021

All rights reserved. No part of this publication may be reproduced or transmitted in any form or by any means, electronic or mechanical, including photocopying, recording, or any other information storage and retrieval system, without the written permission of the publisher.

Internet addresses given in this book were accurate at the time it went to press.

Printed in the United States of America

Published in Hellertown, PA
Cover and interior design and illustrations by Georgia Wilson with Adobe Images

Library of Congress Control Number 2021923369

ISBN #978-1-952481-72-7
2 4 6 8 10 9 7 5 3 1 paperback

www.MomosaPublishing.com

I am so very happy that you have chosen Seven Pearls of Wisdom for Wellness Jewelry Box!

This Seven Pearls Lifebook is the first book in a series
of four, which I hope you will find very useful.
The references to pearls, their formation and growth
are used to build a solid foundation for creating
your personal growth layers and
decision-making as you move forward along your life path.

In this Seven Pearls Lifebook, you will determine
seven core values to begin filling
your "Jewelry Box" with those personal attributes,
which you treasure and will use to live your best life.

Knowing, growing, and using these attributes
with them being the center of who you are
and how you want to represent yourself to others,
inspires a feeling of high self-esteem.

Appreciating your beauty and value
creates an internal environment
where personal growth is most successful.
These values are living and transform as you grow.

Opening yourself to possibilities
makes you eagerly want to live your best,
and success becomes a limitless part of you.

The other Seven Pearls Lifebooks use the
strong foundation that you have built
to set life plans with effective goals
for your spiritual, mental, and physical health
and bring those plans to fruition.

Georgia

A Song

By Lucretia Maria Davidson

*Life is but a troubled ocean,
Hope a meteor, love a flower
Which blossoms in the morning beam,
And withers with the evening hour.*

*Ambition is a dizzy height,
And glory, but a lightning gleam;
Fame is a bubble, dazzling bright,
Which fairest shines in fortune's beam.*

*When clouds and darkness veil the skies,
And sorrow's blast blows loud and chill,
Friendship shall like a rainbow rise,
And softly whisper—peace, be still.*

Table of Contents

Wisdom Comes with Growth and Change

Living Well is…	1
Seven Pearls of Wisdom for Wellness – Jewelry Box	2
Forming Pearls	3
Daisies and Renewal	4
Becoming Butterflies	5
Are You Ready?	6

Recognizing the Valuables in Your Jewelry Box

Filling Your Jewelry Box	7
Life is…	8
Owning A Valuable Jewelry Box	9
What You Will Be Doing in This Lifebook	10
Reason, Season, Or Lifetime	11
Who Are the People in Your Life?	12
Naming Those Who Have Been Important to You	13-14

Stringing Your Personal Seven Pearls of Wisdom

- Purpose – *your life obligation* *15-32*
- Passion – *those indescribable feelings* *33-50*
- Presents – *qualities that are crafted just for you* *51-68*
- Promise – *your worth and integrity* *69-86*
- Power – *your ability to remove any obstacles* *87-104*
- Peace – *the calm that wraps your soul* *105-122*
- Path – *seeing the points beyond the horizon* *123-140*

Personal Mission Statement

- Writing Your Personal Mission Statement *141*
- Brief Value Statements *142*
- My Jewelry Box *143-144*

Acknowledgements *145*

About the Author *146*

Contact Information *147*

Living Well Is...
Changing,
Growing...
and Sharing!

Throughout this Lifebook you will see images of butterflies and daisies in addition to pearls.

This is to remind us of the unique challenges and beauty they each symbolize during different seasons of their lives, as we create the image, we desire for ourselves.

Seven Pearls
of Wisdom for Wellness

*"As a pearl is formed and its layers grow, a rich iridescence begins to glow.
The oyster has taken what was at first an irritation and intrusion and uses it to enrich its value.
How can you coat or frame the changes in your life to harvest beauty, brilliance, and wisdom?"*
~ Susan C. Young

Pearls symbolize feminine beauty and wisdom.
The Pearl, just like wisdom, is usually something rare and precious.
It can begin as an uncomfortable and sometimes unwanted irritant to the receiver.
Over time the knowledge within loses its sharp edge and becomes something of beauty and value.

Pearls represent the best within us, such as honesty, innocence, wisdom and integrity.
They help us to recapture simplicity in our lives.

If we think of something that is said or written as a Pearl of Wisdom,
It means the content sounds very sage or helpful.
The wealth of a Pearl only comes with its discovery and usage.

Wisdom that is not used and shared with others is forever lost.

The Seven Pearls of Wisdom in your Jewelry Box are;

Purpose
Passion
Presents
Promise
Power
Peace
Path

This is your personal Lifebook for you to claim and string your own Seven Pearls of Wisdom.
Remember to wear your Pearls daily to keep their values priceless and treasured.

*"A word of kindness is seldom spoken in vain,
while witty sayings are as easily lost
as the pearls slipping from a broken string."*
~ Unknown

Forming A Pearl

"The Pearl Principle – no inner irritation, no pearl."
~ Surya Das

Pearls are the oldest valuable gem known to mankind, and the only gem that comes from a living animal source. The mystery and symbolism has been passed down through the ages. The value as a means of trade, and show of wealth status on adornments, dates back as early as 2300BC. Divers risked their lives to retrieve this precious gem.

There are basically two main types of Pearls, natural and cultured. Both are formed from mollusks. The process begins as an irritant is introduced into the living mollusk. The mollusk tries to defend itself from the intrusion, and begins to secrete a coating onto the irritant layer upon layer. This coating is called nacre which later becomes the lustrous Pearl. Natural Pearls occur only with influences from nature and are the rarest. Cultured Pearls are farmed by humans introducing the irritants intentionally. With the modern processes, it is increasingly more difficult to determine if a Pearl is natural or cultured.

Gem quality Pearls require an average of 3-4 years to achieve the best nacre coatings. This process requires intense patience to fully develop. Attempts to rush the progression decreases the quality and value of the gem.

Since Pearls are organic in composition, they tend to have individual defects. Certain circumstances affect the characteristics of Pearls. These characteristics include; size, shape, color, pearl type, thickness of the nacre, and luster. Pearls can be formed in fresh or saltwater.

Pearls are not always round, in fact the irregular and imperfect Pearls tend to be more valuable. Pearls are also not smooth; they have a gritty texture, due to the uneven protective covering of the nacre when forming. Exceptional Pearls have a deep, mirror-like surface and a bright and shiny glow. Pearls with low luster have a dull appearance.

"A pearl is a beautiful thing that is produced by an injured life.
It is the tear from an injured oyster.
The treasure of our being in this world
is also produced by an injured life.
If we had not been wounded,
if we had not been injured,
then we will not produce the pearl."
~ Stephen Hoeller

The Daisies

Daisy symbolisms gives us renewal, and return the childlike and simple innocence that we tend to lose as we get older. We feel positive, hopeful, happy, and grateful for all that we have both physically and emotionally. The petals of the daisy remind us of the rays that come from the beautiful sun shining brightly. The center of the daisy reflects all the complexities we are composed of that all put together become our individual and unique self.

The word daisy derives from the Old English meaning of "day's eye" because of a unique characteristic of opening its flower at dawn and closing the petals at dusk. This daily awakening and sleeping reminds us of our daily life cycle rhythm. Daisies follow the path of the sun throughout the day as it desires to draw in the power of the sun for as long as it can.

Symbolism of the daisy includes;
- Purity – especially the white
- Innocence – the white with yellow centers
- Childbirth – often given to new mothers
- New Beginnings – refreshing daily
- Transformation – new life change
- Cheerfulness – positive sunny attitude
- True Love – two flowers blended together

There are thousands of species of daisies in a large variety of sizes, shapes, and colors. They can grow and thrive in many different climates. Daisies grow all year round and are naturally resistant to many diseases and pests which makes them a favorite for many gardeners. Daisies typically begin to flower in early spring. Bloom in early summer, and grow through the end of summer.

A single daisy is actually made of two flowers. The center, or flower head, appears to be one piece, but it is actually a composition of many small flowers. Ray florets are the outer part of the daisy and look like typical petals.

Brightly colored daisies, usually found in South Africa, tend to have longer stems, and darker centers, a favorite for florists. The Shasta daisy is another popular type of daisy that was originally bred in California.

Daisies may be some of the oldest flowers on Earth. Their images have been found in stone carvings dating back to 3,000 BC. This flower was grown for medicinal as well as aesthetic purposes. Oils were extracted to use as an astringent to promote healing. Wild daisy tea is said to be useful for throat ailments. Daisy leaves are edible and many include them in their salads. Those allergic to ragweed may also have difficulties with daisy products.

An Illustration of Change

About the Butterfly

Transformation of a caterpillar to a butterfly has long been used to symbolize the process of change in a person's life from one state of being to another. They may find that their current self is no longer useful, but the alternative may be unbelievable in appearance and insurmountably difficult to attain. The result however, is very well-worth the discomfort. In comparison, this transition of a few weeks with a caterpillar, may take humans a longer period of time. So be patient with the process.

This whole process is called metamorphosis. A butterfly goes through four physical stages in its life cycle. Each stage is very different, and all have a different goal. The entire life cycle process can take from a month to a year, depending on the type of butterfly.

Stage one begins as an egg. The second stage is a caterpillar after it hatches from the egg. Once the caterpillar has emerged, it is extremely hungry and begins to eat ravenously, and grows very quickly. During this hungry stage – from nine to fourteen days – the caterpillar can eat up to 300 times its weight in a single day. The growth occurs so fast that it outgrows its skin, which then must be shed and replaced with new skin. Molting of the skin occurs about four times during this phase. After the last molt, the caterpillar stops eating and prepares to sleep by hanging upside-down from a twig or leaf. Many spin themselves into a cocoon in preparation for the next transformation. Cells within the caterpillar, while it is resting in the cocoon, create the butterfly that will eventually materialize. The emergent butterfly prepares to lift itself through the next phase.

Adult butterflies are pollinators. As they fly from flower-to-flower consuming vital nectar, pollen grains stick to their tiny legs and transfer between flowers to aid in the growth and development of new flowers.

Monarch butterflies offer an amazing story of the butterfly life cycle. Spring migration of the Monarch begins in March as they head north from Central Mexico. They only have a few remaining weeks to live, and the females instinctively lay their eggs as they move north. Northern migration continues from March to June, and the whole process of 2000 miles takes up to three generations to complete. As winter comes, the butterflies begin preparation for the long journey back to Mexico. Amazingly, these new generations of Monarchs know instinctively where to travel via the same route of the previous generations.

"May the next few months be a period of magnificent transformation."
~ UNKNOWN

Are you Ready ...

... to Get Started?

You are ready to begin stringing your Seven Pearls of Wisdom. They should become an important part of your life planning process; use them to design your best self at whatever stage of the path you are on. As with our lives, this pursuit is uniquely suited for your needs and desires. Your pearls are living and growing as you do. Growing, caring for and maintaining the knots between them as a method of reinforcing your pearl importance keeps your other values intact during difficult times when a pearl value could temporarily slip from the strand.

Utilize these seven core values for expansion and moving you forward on your life journey. The solid foundation that you set now will assist you in establishing baselines for designing plans and effective goal setting based on the important core values that you will determine for yourself. The focus is listed and summarized below.

The Seven Core Values in Your Jewelry Box

- *You will define what is important to you,*
- *You will decide how you want to express yourself to others,*
- *You will determine the process of acquiring, nurturing and enhancing the attributes of the values you determine.*

You should take your time to carefully look deep within yourself as you complete the worksheets. It is useful to collaborate with a partner to see if what you feel is an accurate portrayal of yourself – a sounding board. The worksheets are intended to promote thought, not to tell you what you should do. The answers for you are within you and ready to be discovered, polished, and used in your daily life.

Remember to enjoy the process. Celebrate successes as well as challenges. They are there for a reason. Transitions and renewals are not meant to be punitive. As the daisies you see throughout the pages each day offers a new beginning to absorb open and, just like the butterfly the discomfort will be well worth the effort because you will be leading the beautiful life you desire.

Filling My Jewelry Box

Life is an opportunity, benefit from it.
Life is beauty, admire it.
Life is bliss, taste it.
Life is a dream, realize it.
Life is a challenge, meet it.
Life is a duty, complete it.
Life is a game, play it.
Life is a promise, fulfill it.
Life is sorrow, overcome it.
Life is a song, sing it.
Life is a struggle, accept it.
Life is a tragedy, confront it.
Life is an adventure, dare it.
Life is luck, make it.
Life is too precious, do not destroy it.
Life is life, fight for it.

~ *Mother Teresa*

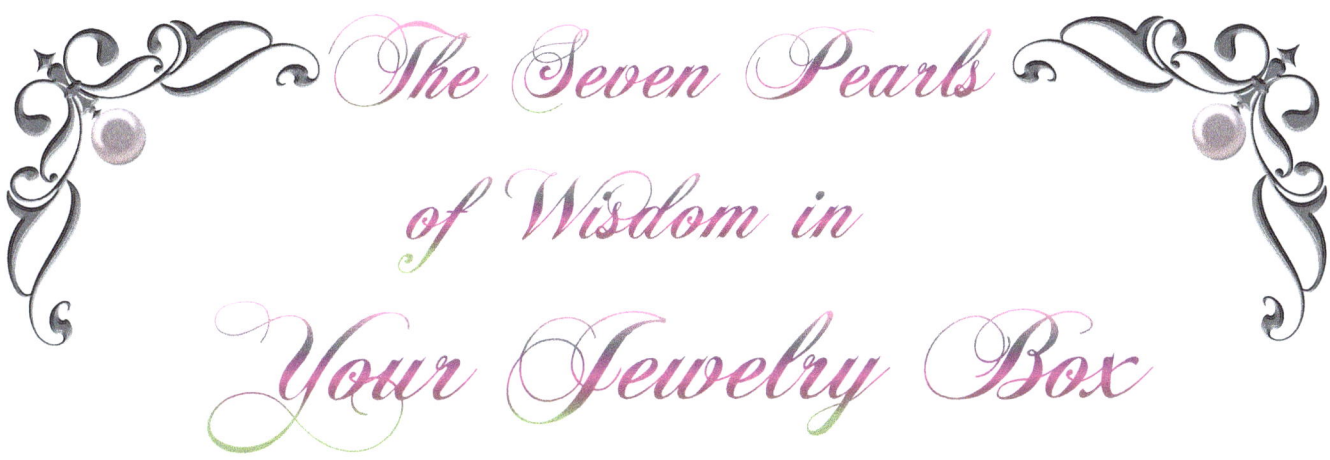

The Seven Pearls of Wisdom in Your Jewelry Box

Our jewelry boxes hold those gems we treasure, whether for their beauty to us, or for their sentimental value. We enjoy wearing these gems daily or on special occasions. They accessorize our wardrobes, and complete the image we want to portray with the outfit we have chosen. Your Seven Pearls of Wisdom for Wellness are those beautiful Pearl gems that become our core values that we wear daily. We may have other valuable gems, but these Pearls can be worn at any and all times, either alone or in conjunction with other gems.

The best Pearls are knotted to secure them, and keep them from all falling from the strand should any area become compromised. Periodic care and maintenance is necessary for their beauty, luster, value, and strand integrity. One of the best ways to maintain the luster is to wear them daily. Our body oils enhance the luster. Our values require the same care and attention to optimize their usefulness in maintaining our well-being.

We all have an internal moral compass whose sole purpose is to move our actions back to where we should be, when we find we are losing our way. The message may come to us as a nagging nudge that just won't go away, and if needed, it may present as an indiscreet shove or shout to get us to pay attention. To redirect ourselves, we just have to be open to listening and hearing those messages, and following the guidance. It is all in our best interest.

The spirit of those messages comes to us throughout our lives. Primarily, the guidance comes to us by what we are taught by our influencers, and also through our experiences, whether they are positive or challenging. Influencers may certainly be our family members and friends, but they also may be people we respect and admire as they carry themselves in a manner desire to emulate.

Our personal world is forever changing, and if we allow ourselves to never stop learning, we will grow and polish those core values that make us our best person. If the voice is not always the same, it is because it changes as our principles are redefined – we grow as we know. The process of change is often initially uncomfortable and possibly scary, but truly worth it in the end and can become our new comfort.

What Are You Going to Do?

To claim and define your seven core principles in this section of your Lifebook, take your time as you go through the activities for each Pearl. Think carefully about the answers to questions. There is no wrong answer, the right answer is what it means to you. They can help you with your journey toward discovery, but they are not meant to tell you what you should do. The intent is to stimulate your thoughts about what you want, how you can get what you need, and how you can be of best service to yourself and others. Core values design a blueprint for your life. They are necessary for putting action to your beliefs about what is important to you. You may have more than seven values, but the Seven Pearls chosen lay a strong foundation for living well. You define how they are valuable to you and how to acquire, grow, nourish, and hold them within you.

Work through each Pearl in the order that works best for you, and at the pace that is comfortable for you. You will find recurring thoughts and ideas that connect and overlap the values. This is because all aspects of who we are, should connect to make us whole and complete.

If you have the Pearl already, think about how it came to you. This can help you in finding your strengths or resources for other areas. If there are values you see as important to you, but you don't have the attributes you need to bring them into your life yet, the activities offer opportunities to think of ways to make them a part of your being. Use the brainstorming pages to help you visualize each value in your life and what you need to bring it to reality.

You may find it helpful to partner with someone you trust as a sounding board for what you are finding. Ideally, this person should honestly, and compassionately, let you know if what you are thinking is what you are projecting as what you desire.

When you have established all Seven Pearls, write your Personal Mission Statement using all seven core values. In your mission commit to daily wearing, enhancing, repairing, and sharing something about your Pearls. All of them do not need to be touched daily, but remain displayed by your actions.

Knowing where you are going, makes reaching your life journey destination so much more exciting, and with minimal need for rerouting.

Most importantly, as usual, enjoy the process. It is not punishment, it makes you better!

Reason, Season, or Lifetime

People come into your life for a Reason, a Season or a Lifetime.
When you figure out which it is, you know exactly what to do.

When someone is in your life for a *REASON*,
It is usually to meet a need you have expressed outwardly or inwardly.
They have come to assist you through a difficulty,
Or to provide you with guidance and support,
To aid you physically, emotionally, or even spiritually.

They may seem like a godsend to you, and they are.
They are there for the reason you need them to be.
Then, without any wrong doing on your part or at an inconvenient time,
This person will say or do something to bring the relationship to an end.

Sometimes they die. Sometimes they just walk away.
Sometimes they act up and force you to take a stand.
What we must realize is that our need has been met,
our desire fulfilled; their work is done.
The prayer you sent up has been answered and it is now time to move on.

When people come into your life for a *SEASON*,
It is because your turn has come to share, grow, or learn.
They may bring you an experience of peace or make you laugh.
They may teach you something you have never done.

They usually give you an unbelievable amount of joy.
Believe it! It is real! But, only for a season.
And like Spring turns to Summer and Summer to Fall,
The season eventually ends.

LIFETIME relationships teach you lifetime lessons;
Those things you must build upon in order to have a solid emotional foundation.
Your job is to accept the lesson, love the person anyway;
And put what you have learned to use in all other relationships and areas in your life.

It is said that love is blind but friendship is clairvoyant.
Thank you for being part of my life,
Whether you were a Reason, a Season or a Lifetime.

~ Unknown

Who Are The People In Your Life?

We often encounter people who have an aura of that "special something" that we admire or draws us to them. The qualities they possess are attractive to us, and we would love to have that same attribute within us. We would love it if they could mentor us – maybe they could if we would only ask!

On the other hand, we may know people who are in roles or positions that we feel are a bad fit for that which they are charged. We witness them negatively impacting our life or the lives of others. We may feel the actions or behaviors of those whom they oversee are not being best served.

Both are examples of influencers that could be beneficial to you for stringing your Seven Pearls. These influencers may be aware of their impact on you, and they may not, either way their actions add to your personal growth.

Look around you, seek out those who provide those sparks to becoming your best person, and better yet, use the input to propel you forward with ambition. Refer back to those you have identified in the following worksheets as helpful as you work through each of your core values for inspiration.

A major part of the joy and meaning of receiving any life gift is the commitment to share it with others so that the bounty just keeps on giving and growing.

Asking an admirable person for their assistance is not a weakness, it is taking advantage of a growth opportunity. Let them know about the difference they have made within you if at all possible. It may be an element of their own personal life path to extend what they have to others – you could be helping them grow!

Naming Those Who Have Been Important in Your Life.

Name of Person or Source	R S L	Description of Influence	Aware?

The influencers came into your life for: R – Reason, S – Season, L – Lifetime

Name of Person or Source	R S L	Description of Influence	Aware?

The influencers came into your life for: R – Reason, S – Season, L – Lifetime

Purpose

*"The purpose of life is not to be happy.
It is to be useful, to be honorable,
to be compassionate, to have it make some
difference that you have lived, and lived well."*
~ *Ralph Waldo Emerson*

If you do not understand your Purpose, you may feel as if there is something missing in your life. You are trying to put together a puzzle, and it appears that the pieces you need to complete the picture are missing, or do not fit. You may be asking yourself what it is you are not doing, just why you are here, and what is it you are supposed to be doing in service to others.

It is frustrating to find yourself stuck in an unfulfilling situation that you know is not intended for you, but you see others around you appearing to be living their dreams and ask yourself. Why not me?

When trying to find your Purpose, it is imperative that you not waste your time comparing yourself with others and fearing how others will react to what you are compelled to do. This is your destiny, and although you can sometimes take others with you, the ultimate destination is yours. This is the peace your soul is seeking, and as long as your intentions have integrity, this is a part of your character.

Remain aware of those messages that stir personal emotions for action. You must openly accept your gifts — what you are good at — and be willing to grow as you move along. Sometimes a disturbing experience can create a need within you to set things right. When you willingly make sacrifices to make that happen, that is Purpose.

How can you find your Purpose?

- Visualize yourself reaching your dream
- Reach out to others who can help you
- Try new things
- Push through discomfort
- Investigate the reason for recurring thoughts
- Keep your goals foremost in your thoughts

Potential challenges...

- Fear of making a mistake
- Impatience with the rate of progress
- Negative self-talk
- Unwillingness to acknowledge opportunities

Benefits to you...

- You feel great about what you are doing
- You are energized
- Life makes sense
- Creativity is released
- Best use of your valuable time

*"It is not easy for any of us, but what of that?
We must have perseverance and above all
confidence in ourselves.
We must believe we are gifted for something,
and this thing must be attained."*

~ Marie Curie

Wise Purpose Words

What are the meanings of these proverbs to you?

"A man knows no more of any purpose than he practices."
~ FRENCH

"When silent men speak, they speak to the purpose."
~ GERMAN

"Accomplishment of purpose is better than making a profit."
~ HAUSA

"Having achieved your purpose, seek not to undo what has been done."
~ LATIN

"He is wise to no purpose, who is not wise for himself."
~ LATIN

"We are all visitors to this time, this place. We are just passing through. Our purpose here is to learn, to grow, to love...and then we return home."
~ ABORIGINAL

"Battle doesn't need a purpose; the battle is its own purpose."
~ TRADITIONAL

"Speak little and to the purpose."
~ TRADITIONAL

"The purpose sanctifies the means."
~ DUTCH

"There are hidden purposes behind an act."
~ INDONESIAN

"Better to say nothing, than to say something not to the purpose."
~ ENGLISH

"The secret to success is consistency."
~ ENGLISH

"Let your bargain suit you purpose."
~ IRISH

"Don't question a blind man for buying a mirror, it must serve him some purpose."
~ AFRICAN

"What does it matter that one bowl is dark and the other pale, if each is of good design and serves its purpose well."
~ HOPI

Some questions and thoughts about your Purpose to consider...

- ✔ Where would you love to be?

- ✔ What is your calling?

- ✔ When is choice not a sacrifice to you at all?

- ✔ What opportunities have you been avoiding?

- ✔ What keeps you awake thinking you should be doing?

- ✔ What is your heart telling you?

- ✔ What do you want to leave as your legacy?

...Tea and Thoughts...

✔ *What feels just right?*

✔ *When do you feel at ease?*

✔ *What would living to your full potential look like?*

✔ *What is missing from your life?*

✔ *What do you want to achieve in your lifetime?*

✔ *What is important to you?*

✔ *Who makes you feel satisfied?*

...and More Growth!

✔ What are you drawn to?
___
___
___

✔ What can you do to improve the life of others?
___
___
___

✔ What piques your curiosity?
___
___
___

✔ How can you make a difference?
___
___
___

✔ What do you want to learn more about?
___
___
___

✔ When do you feel trapped?
___
___
___

✔ What motivates you to do more?
___
___
___

How your life might be affected by not understanding your Purpose

- No drive or action
- Disconnect from self or others
- No sense of direction
- Poor life decision-making
- Inability to set effective goals
- Low energy
- Not open to possibilities
- Stagnant learning
- Feelings of insecurity

Some key words describing the opposite of Purpose

inefficiency	triviality	inadequacy	hopelessness	futility
meaninglessness	emptiness	unproductiveness	worthlessness	uselessness
disorganization	lack	unimportance	poverty	inability
inefficacy	insignificance	fruitlessness	idleness	weakness
ignorance	pointlessness	incapacity	need	ineptness

My feelings about not understanding my Purpose…

_____
_____
_____
_____
_____
_____
_____
_____
_____

Words Are Valuable and Meaningful

PURPOSE DEFINITIONS

- Expected outcome that guides a planned action
- What something is used for
- Having determination to do or achieve something
- Strong commitment to a cause

Highlight the words that express the meaning of Purpose to you.

hope	craving	challenge
consciousness	influence	vision
mission	ingenuity	dream
determination	substance	intensity
incentive	design	attitude
resolve	heart	initiative
aim	persistence	desire
enlightenment	certainty	inclination
lifework	plan	vision
expertise	devotion	ambition
faith	commitment	service
initiative	visualization	tenacity
cause	destiny	blueprint
thrust	interest	duty
doggedness	drive	grit
spirit	aspiration	instinct
dedication	endeavor	longing
inspiration	direction	reason
awareness	fortitude	character
motion	inclination	enjoyment
essence	obligation	message
entrepreneurship	decision	connection
assignment	responsibility	foundation
vocation	concern	pleasure
pursuit	necessity	mastery

*Now go back and choose the five **most meaningful** words to describe Purpose attributes you would like to have on your Pearl Strand and circle the butterfly beside them.*

*Describe each chosen Purpose attribute you want on your
Pearl Strand, and why they are necessary
for your personal growth and well-being.
Then rate them 1-5 in order of importance to you.*

Layering My Purpose Pearl

What do I need?

Why do I want this?

When can I get started?

Layering My Purpose Pearl

Where can I get what I need?

How can I get what I need?

Who can help me?

Defining Your Purpose Value

Purpose Attribute	If you have the attribute, how and when did you receive it?
	What were the influences that helped you?

Purpose Attribute	If you have the attribute, how and when did you receive it?
	What were the influences that helped you?

Purpose Attribute	If you have the attribute, how and when did you receive it?
	What were the influences that helped you?

Purpose Attribute	If you have the attribute, how and when did you receive it?
	What were the influences that helped you?

Purpose Attribute	If you have the attribute, how and when did you receive it?
	What were the influences that helped you?

Growing and Enhancing Your Purpose Values

Want Value ○ **Enhance Value** ○ *Circle beside...* *whether you want* *to add the attribute* *to your life,* *Or* *Want to grow more* *attributes of the* *value that you have.*	*What is needed to string this pearl or add to its luster?* *How can you create or maintain the knot of this pearl?*
Want Value ○ **Enhance Value** ○ *Circle beside...* *whether you want* *to add the attribute* *to your life,* *Or* *Want to grow more* *attributes of the* *value that you have.*	*What is needed to string this pearl or add to its luster?* *How can you create or maintain the knot of this pearl?*
Want Value ○ **Enhance Value** ○ *Circle beside...* *whether you want* *to add the attribute* *to your life,* *Or* *Want to grow more* *attributes of the* *value that you have.*	*What is needed to string this pearl or add to its luster?* *How can you create or maintain the knot of this pearl?*
Want Value ○ **Enhance Value** ○ *Circle beside...* *whether you want* *to add the attribute* *to your life,* *Or* *Want to grow more* *attributes of the* *value that you have.*	*What is needed to string this pearl or add to its luster?* *How can you create or maintain the knot of this pearl?*
Want Value ○ **Enhance Value** ○ *Circle beside...* *whether you want* *to add the attribute* *to your life,* *Or* *Want to grow more* *attributes of the* *value that you have.*	*What is needed to string this pearl or add to its luster?* *How can you create or maintain the knot of this pearl?*

Making It Happen!

I am doing the work to discover my Purpose.

Task	How it will help me.	Start Date	Complete Date - C / Or Ongoing - O

Task	How it will help me.	Start Date	Complete Date - C Or Ongoing - O
			C O
			C O
			C O
			C O
			C O
			C O
			C O
			C O
			C O
			C O
			C O
			C O
			C O
			C O
			C O
			C O
			C O
			C O
			C O
			C O
			C O

The Pearls of Wisdom in My Jewelry Box

My Purpose Pearl Commitment

I will use the attributes that I have determined to be essential for becoming the person I aspire to be by…

_____
_____
_____
_____
_____

and, furthermore I commit to maintaining the cycle of wisdom by sharing my knowledge with others by…

_____
_____
_____
_____
_____

Passion

"Only passions, great passions can elevate the soul to great things."
~ Denis Diderot

Have you ever found yourself awakened during the night with a great idea that you need to write down right away while the thought is fresh? Likewise, do you know what you would do, without any thought, if there were no obstacles such as time or money? If you have had these thoughts, you are uncovering your Passion.

Your Passion is what you enjoy doing the most and what drives you well beyond your comfort zone. You are willing to do the work – but it does not feel like work – to learn more and more about it. You are smiling inside and out while sharing what you love with others, and it never becomes tiring.

The cause may be so compelling that it is not only motivating but it is also challenging, and when you try distancing from the desire you are continually drawn back to it. The emotional connection is so intense. You are alive, you want to do it, and you are really good at it! Passion is the catalyst for innovation and makes what seems impossible a reality long before it actually comes to fruition. Your senses are extremely heightened.

Om the other hand, maybe you feel that you have not discovered what your passion is. Believe it is there – within you – you just have not recognized it yet. Be patient, keep trying new things, listen to your intuition, and be open to all possibilities. Discovery can come anywhere and very unexpectedly. Many different facets may come together as one or many Passions can interconnect.

How can you follow your Passion?

- What thoughts awaken you or keep you up?
- Write down driving thoughts immediately
- Seek out mentors
- Truly believe you can make a change
- Partner with like-minded people
- Pursue your interests

Potential challenges…

- Ignoring those mental nudges
- Wasting your wisdom
- Fear of growing – feeling overwhelmed
- Accepting negative messages as truth

Benefits to you…

- You are enjoying life
- Challenges become learning experiences
- You desire to share your wisdom with others
- Others seek you out for your knowledge
- It becomes a part of your being

"The most powerful weapon on Earth is a human soul on fire."
~ Ferdinand Foch

Wise Passion Words

What are the meanings of these proverbs to you?

- *"It is not the greatest beauties that inspire the most profound passion."*
  ~ FRENCH

- *"Lust of power is the strongest of all passions."*
  ~ LATIN

- *"When passion enters at the beginning wisdom goes out at the end."*
  ~ SPANISH

- *"If passion drives let reason hold the reins."*
  ~ AMERICAN

- *"Diligence is a great teacher."*
  ~ ARABIAN

"Nothing is so difficult that diligence cannot master it."
~ MALAGASY

"Diligence is the beginning of brilliance."
~ INDONESIAN

"Diligence is the mistress of success."
~ ENGLISH

"To endure what is unendurable is true endurance."
~ JAPANESE

"A year's harvest counts on spring, a man's success counts on diligence."
~ CHINESE

"Persistence will count more than force."
~ AMERICAN

"Life is not a continuum of pleasant choices, but inevitable problems that call for strength, determination and hard work."
~ INDIAN

"The key to all things is determination."
~ ARABIC

"Don't underestimate the determination of a quiet person."
~ AFRICAN

"Diligence is the vehicle on the paths of mountains of books, endurance is the vessel of the course of the seas of learning."
~ CHINESE

Some questions and thoughts about your Passion to consider...

✔ What does the world need?

✔ What brings the biggest smile to your face?

✔ Who would you love to meet?

✔ What would make you a better person?

✔ What compels you to improve things?

✔ What awakens your spirit?

✔ What are your strongest desires?

...Tea and Thoughts...

✔ What are you ready to do when the time is right?
___

✔ What are your dreams?
___

✔ What distracts you?
___

✔ When do you feel at your best?
___

✔ What makes you high on life?
___

✔ What makes you sing out loud?
___

✔ What angers you?
___

...and More Growth!

- ✔ What do you love to do?
  _____
  _____

- ✔ What needs to be set right?
  _____
  _____
  _____

- ✔ What would be beyond imagination?
  _____
  _____
  _____

- ✔ What makes you feel fearless?
  _____
  _____
  _____

- ✔ What never feels wrong?
  _____
  _____
  _____

- ✔ What do you never have second thoughts about doing?
  _____
  _____
  _____

- ✔ Who would you love to mentor you?
  _____
  _____
  _____

How your life might be affected by not knowing your Passion

- Feeling lost
- Unsure who you are and where you want to be
- Unmotivated for growth and change
- One day just runs into another
- No enthusiasm
- Feeling fearful
- Feeling negative
- Easily discouraged
- Uncertain future
- Mentally foggy
- Unchallenged

Some key words describing the opposite of Passion

indifference	coolness	stoicism	frigidity	revulsion
nonchalance	stiffness	inaction	disregard	loathing
apathy	detachment	unfeeling	reluctance	stoniness
reticence	idleness	aversion	antipathy	unconcern
passiveness	negligence	disinterest	coldness	dread

My feelings about not having a life Passion ...

_____
_____
_____
_____
_____
_____
_____

Words Are Valuable and Meaningful

PASSION DEFINITIONS

- *Intense emotional pursuit of a belief or desire*
- *Something that creates an intense interest and enthusiasm*
- *Quest for an uncontrollable urge*

Highlight the words that express the meaning of Passion to you.

fire	emotion	fortitude
appetite	rapture	intensity
inspiration	ardor	vehemence
partiality	fierceness	allegiance
craze	obsession	preoccupation
intrigue	insistence	fixation
niche	interest	mission
zealousness	flame	commitment
dedication	aspiration	absorption
hankering	mania	elation
sentiment	devotion	feeling
desire	fascination	momentum
ebullience	longing	adoration
fever	delight	spellbinding
madness	itch	immersion
drive	eagerness	determination
seduction	spirit	loyalty
impulse	fervor	gusto
enthusiasm	stimulation	sensation
initiative	addiction	excitement
yearning	inclination	thrill
ache	thirst	fanaticism
frenzy	doggedness	storm
wishing	enchantment	obligation
exhilaration	zest	impetus

*Now go back and choose the five **most meaningful** words to describe Passion attributes you would like to have on your Pearl Strand and circle the butterfly beside them.*

42

*Describe each chosen Passion attribute you want on your
Pearl Strand, and why they are necessary
for your personal growth and well-being.
Then rate them 1-5 in order of importance to you.*

Layering My Passion Pearl

What do I need?

Why do I want this?

When can I get started?

Layering My Passion Pearl

Where can I get what I need?

How can I get what I need?

Who can help me?

Defining Your Passion Value

Passion Attribute	If you have the attribute, how and when did you receive it?
	What were the influences that helped you?

Passion Attribute	If you have the attribute, how and when did you receive it?
	What were the influences that helped you?

Passion Attribute	If you have the attribute, how and when did you receive it?
	What were the influences that helped you?

Passion Attribute	If you have the attribute, how and when did you receive it?
	What were the influences that helped you?

Passion Attribute	If you have the attribute, how and when did you receive it?
	What were the influences that helped you?

Growing and Enhancing Your Passion Values

Want Value ⬤ **Enhance Value** ⬤ *Circle beside...* *whether you want* *to add the attribute* *to your life,* *Or* *Want to grow more* *attributes of the* *value that you have.*	*What is needed to string this pearl or add to its luster?* *How can you create or maintain the knot of this pearl?*
Want Value ⬤ **Enhance Value** ⬤ *Circle beside...* *whether you want* *to add the attribute* *to your life,* *Or* *Want to grow more* *attributes of the* *value that you have.*	*What is needed to string this pearl or add to its luster?* *How can you create or maintain the knot of this pearl?*
Want Value ⬤ **Enhance Value** ⬤ *Circle beside...* *whether you want* *to add the attribute* *to your life,* *Or* *Want to grow more* *attributes of the* *value that you have.*	*What is needed to string this pearl or add to its luster?* *How can you create or maintain the knot of this pearl?*
Want Value ⬤ **Enhance Value** ⬤ *Circle beside...* *whether you want* *to add the attribute* *to your life,* *Or* *Want to grow more* *attributes of the* *value that you have.*	*What is needed to string this pearl or add to its luster?* *How can you create or maintain the knot of this pearl?*
Want Value ⬤ **Enhance Value** ⬤ *Circle beside...* *whether you want* *to add the attribute* *to your life,* *Or* *Want to grow more* *attributes of the* *value that you have.*	*What is needed to string this pearl or add to its luster?* *How can you create or maintain the knot of this pearl?*

Making It Happen!

I am doing the work to discover my Passion.

Task	How it will help me.	Start Date	Complete Date — C Or Ongoing - O

Task	How it will help me.	Start Date	Complete Date - C Or Ongoing - O
			C O
			C O
			C O
			C O
			C O
			C O
			C O
			C O
			C O
			C O
			C O
			C O
			C O
			C O
			C O
			C O
			C O
			C O
			C O
			C O
			C O
			C O

The Pearls of Wisdom in My Jewelry Box

My Passion Pearl Commitment

I will use the attributes that I have determined to be essential for becoming the person I aspire to be by…

_____
_____
_____
_____
_____

and, furthermore I commit to maintaining the cycle of wisdom by sharing my knowledge with others by…

_____
_____
_____
_____
_____

Presents

"The meaning of life is to find your gift, the purpose of life is to give it away."
~ Pablo Picasso

Your Presents are those attributes that have been selected just for you. They are those unique skills and talents you possess. You may already know what they are but have not optimized them. You also may not recognize what has been gifted to you. You could be overlooking the valuable knowledge you have already that could help you on your life path.

Talents come naturally to you. Tasks can be performed with little or no extra effort, and you enjoy doing them. The talent may require enhanced training and coaching to maintain peak performance, but the results for you are very rewarding and others see the ability in you. You can discover your talents by expanding your range of information and trying new things that you may have overlooked as possibilities.

When something just seems to come to you and makes sense without your really thinking about how it happens, it is a special skill. You can see improvements or different ways of doing things that others cannot even fathom. This is the creative side of you. You can see something in nothing; you are open to possibilities becoming realities; and you have the ability to make it happen. Others are amazed at your end result.

Be aware of what you may be called upon to do because others see you as the right person for the task. The wonderful thing is that it is never too late to receive your Presents. They may appear during challenging situations and manifest themselves in your ability to seamlessly move through the difficulty.

Your Presents can open doors of opportunity and allow you to create new roads on your life path that were not there before. Presents are not just for receiving! You have a responsibility to give to others as well – it all moves full-circle.

How can you receive your Presents?

- Recognize your importance
- Know what is uniquely special about you
- Expand on skills you have
- Recognize how you influence successes
- Ask other what they see in you
- Take a class in something unfamiliar to you

Potential challenges…

- Unwillingness to reach outside of what you know
- Feeling it is too late to start something new
- Fear of failure
- Procrastination with using your talents

Benefits to you…

- Finding new ways of doing things
- You are in action mode for progress
- You are giving to others
- You get out of your own way
- You see things more positively

*"I've always known I was gifted,
which is not the easiest thing
in the world for a person to know,
because you're not responsible for your gift,
only for what you do with it."*
~ Hazel Scott

Wise Presents Words

What are the meanings of these proverbs to you?

"Each day provides its own gift."
~ AMERICAN

_____
_____
_____

"Gifts are often losses."
~ ITALIAN

_____
_____
_____

"Promises must not fill the place of gifts."
~ LATIN

_____
_____
_____

"Secret gifts are openly rewarded."
~ DANISH

_____
_____
_____

"Gifts dissolve rocks."
~ TRADITIONAL

_____
_____
_____

"Inner peace and love are the greatest gifts."
~ SIOUX

"The best gifts are those that expect no return."
~ NORWEGIAN

"Blessings are better than wealth."
~ SWAHILI

"Tribulations and blessings, if you have them, keep them."
~ SICILIAN

"Greater qualities are needed to bear good fortune than bad."
~ FRENCH

"Don't look for more honor than your learning merits."
~ JEWISH

"What force may not do, ingenuity may."
~ SPANISH

"Cleverness is better than strength."
~ AFRICAN

"He who prizes little things, is worthy of great ones."
~ GERMAN

"Forget the favors you have given; remember those received."
~ CHINESE

Some questions and thoughts about your Presents to consider...

- ✔ *How do you learn best?*

- ✔ *How do you appreciate what has been given to you?*

- ✔ *What is easy for you to learn or do?*

- ✔ *How well do you celebrate those you love?*

- ✔ *How do others describe you?*

- ✔ *What are you proud of?*

- ✔ *What is special about you?*

...Tea and Thoughts...

✔ *What are you known for?*

✔ *What are your interests and hobbies?*

✔ *How do feel about challenges?*

✔ *What would you love to learn to do?*

✔ *What has become better with time?*

✔ *If you could invent something, what would it be?*

✔ *What surprises you that you do well?*

...and More Growth!

✔ *How do you release your creativity?*
_____
_____
_____

✔ *What are you optimistic about?*
_____
_____
_____

✔ *What was your most memorable event?*
_____
_____
_____

✔ *How do you find solution to problems?*
_____
_____
_____

✔ *What is your most productive time of day?*
_____
_____
_____

✔ *What have you proudly accomplished?*
_____
_____
_____

✔ *What do others know you will be able to do?*
_____
_____
_____

How your life might be affected by not receiving your Presents

- Having strengths that are not being used
- Talents not fully developed
- Not reaching you full potential
- Trapped where you do not want to be
- Missing out on enjoyable experiences
- Feeling bored
- Feeling of failure
- Underachieving
- Missed opportunities for growth
- Not connecting with positive influences
- Not seeing your Purpose or Path
- Not seeing your uniqueness
- Feeling fearful

Some key words describing the opposite of Presents

loaded down	inconveniences	nuisances	limits	burdens
disfavor	limits	bothers	liabilities	obstacles
confusion	constraints	inhibits	encumbrances	fogginess
obstruction	dullness	blocks	scourges	strains
disadvantages	faults	Impediments	banes	failings

My feelings about not accepting the Presents meant for me…

_____
_____
_____
_____
_____
_____

Words Are Valuable and Meaningful

PRESENTS DEFINITIONS
- Received without compensation
- Natural abilities or qualities
- Given as a gift
- Benefits gained from access to something

Highlight the words that express the meaning of Presents to you.

bonuses	charity	invitations
instincts	incentives	accomplishments
freedom	adeptness	cleverness
keenness	sensitivity	souvenirs
abilities	qualities	bounty
remembrances	enthusiasm	graces
favors	smarts	expertise
attributes	character	influences
rewards	largesse	amenities
generosity	keenness	knacks
contributions	artistry	flair
perks	acuity	prizes
support	specialties	resources
aptitudes	considerations	benefactions
indulgence	liberality	privilege
endowments	talents	strengths
pleasures	awards	donations
value	skills	wealth
fluency	blessings	advantage
inclination	pledges	offerings
capabilities	virtue	craftsmanship
sharpness	fluency	usefulness
gifts	worth	brilliance
expression	capability	savvy
bequeaths	tributes	generosities

*Now go back and choose the five **most meaningful** words to describe attributes of presents you would like to have on your Pearl Strand and circle the butterfly beside them.*

60

*Describe each chosen Presents attribute you want on your
Pearl Strand, and why they are necessary
for your personal growth and well-being.
Then rate them 1-5 in order of importance to you.*

☐ _____

_____

_____

_____

☐ _____

_____

_____

_____

☐ _____

_____

_____

_____

☐ _____

_____

_____

_____

☐ _____

_____

_____

_____

Layering My Presents Pearl

What do I need?

Why do I want this?

When can I get started?

Layering My Presents Pearl

Where can I get what I need?

How can I get what I need?

Who can help me?

Defining Your Presents Value

Presents Attribute	If you have the attribute, how and when did you receive it?
	What were the influences that helped you?
Presents Attribute	If you have the attribute, how and when did you receive it?
	What were the influences that helped you?
Presents Attribute	If you have the attribute, how and when did you receive it?
	What were the influences that helped you?
Presents Attribute	If you have the attribute, how and when did you receive it?
	What were the influences that helped you?
Presents Attribute	If you have the attribute, how and when did you receive it?
	What were the influences that helped you?

Growing and Enhancing Your Presents Values

Want Value ○ **Enhance Value** ○ *Circle beside...* *whether you want* *to add the attribute* *to your life,* *Or* *Want to grow more* *attributes of the* *value that you have.*	*What is needed to string this pearl or add to its luster?* *How can you create or maintain the knot of this pearl?*
Want Value ○ **Enhance Value** ○ *Circle beside...* *whether you want* *to add the attribute* *to your life,* *Or* *Want to grow more* *attributes of the* *value that you have.*	*What is needed to string this pearl or add to its luster?* *How can you create or maintain the knot of this pearl?*
Want Value ○ **Enhance Value** ○ *Circle beside...* *whether you want* *to add the attribute* *to your life,* *Or* *Want to grow more* *attributes of the* *value that you have.*	*What is needed to string this pearl or add to its luster?* *How can you create or maintain the knot of this pearl?*
Want Value ○ **Enhance Value** ○ *Circle beside...* *whether you want* *to add the attribute* *to your life,* *Or* *Want to grow more* *attributes of the* *value that you have.*	*What is needed to string this pearl or add to its luster?* *How can you create or maintain the knot of this pearl?*
Want Value ○ **Enhance Value** ○ *Circle beside...* *whether you want* *to add the attribute* *to your life,* *Or* *Want to grow more* *attributes of the* *value that you have.*	*What is needed to string this pearl or add to its luster?* *How can you create or maintain the knot of this pearl?*

Making It Happen!

I am doing the work to unwrap my Presents.

Task	How it will help me.	Start Date	Complete Date – C Or Ongoing – O

Task	How it will help me.	Start Date	Complete Date C Or Ongoing - O

The Pearls of Wisdom in My Jewelry Box

My Presents Pearl Commitment

I will use the attributes that I have determined to be essential for becoming the person I aspire to be by…

_____
_____
_____
_____
_____

and, furthermore I commit to maintaining the cycle of wisdom by sharing my knowledge with others by…

_____
_____
_____
_____
_____

Promise

"If you are not good for yourself, how can you be good for others?"

~ *Spanish Proverb*

When you have Promise, others see the potential for achieving excellence in you and your efforts. Your attributes create an image that is far beyond the average expectation. You have demonstrated the ability to complete and optimize tasks as assigned.

One of the strongest and most impactful commitments you can make to yourself and others is a Promise. Your words give hope. The person receiving the Promise feels valued and assured that you will not let them down. This vow is more potent than *I can*, *I may*, or *I will*. *I Promise*, holds power, emotion and connection with the receiver.

Promises to yourself are very sacred and build self-esteem. You see yourself as worthy of the attention. You are doing something as a result of a strong desire, not because you should but because you deserve it. Unfortunately, it has been instilled in us too often to guilt ourselves for doing things that make us better. We forget that strengthening our bodies and spirit allows us more means to help others. You cannot give what you do not have.

Unfulfilled Promises break the bonds you have established with yourself and others, and the trust in your words is devalued. This connection may never be reestablished or may remain doubtful and tense. It is therefore vital to not overextend yourself to prevent unrealistic expectations. Sometimes the answer to a request must be no, and that is the sincerest answer that may be given. It is an honest response to what you cannot offer.

How can you live with Promise?

- Relationships with others are mutually respectful
- You have integrity
- Live up to your own expectations
- Embrace your life in the moment
- What you say matches what you feel
- Know what is right for you

Potential challenges…

- Comparing yourself to others
- Unrealistic expectations
- Feeling vulnerable
- Feeling selfish for taking care of yourself

Benefits to you…

- Self-acceptance
- Living your own values
- Self-discovery
- Confidence in communicating who you are
- Ability to adapt to change

*"I am neither especially clever,
nor especially gifted,
I am only very, very curious."*
~ Albert Einstein

Wise Promise Words

What are the meanings of these proverbs to you?

"A small gift is better than a great promise."
~ GERMAN

"Sincerity gives wings to power."
~ LATIN

"A half-truth is a whole-lie."
~ YIDDISH

"Promises are like the full moon, if they are not kept at once they diminish day by day."
~ GERMAN

"A promise is a cloud; fulfillment is rain."
~ ARABIAN

"*Promises must not fill the place of gifts.*"
~ LATIN

"*Promises make friends but it is performance that keeps them.*"
~ GERMAN

"*Want and necessity break faith and oaths.*"
~ DANISH

"*An agreement is a kind of debt.*"
~ MOROCCAN

"*Truth's best ornament is nakedness.*"
~ GERMAN

"Keeping a secret is a commitment."
~ ARABIC

"A true word needs no oath."
~ TURKISH

"Open your eyes and ears when contracting, because the agreed upon circumstances mean a lot."
~ SICILIAN

"Where there is negotiation, there is hope for agreement."
~ AFRICAN

"Another's mouth cannot take an oath for you."
~ KIKUYU

Some questions and thoughts about your Promise to consider...

- ✔ *What things are mysterious to you?*

- ✔ *Describe how you are kind and forgiving to yourself?*

- ✔ *How could you do what you love?*

- ✔ *How do you release toxic people from your life?*

- ✔ *How do you keep your conversations positive?*

- ✔ *What do you question?*

- ✔ *How often do you listen to your inner voice?*

Tea and thoughts...

✔ How important is integrity to you?

✔ How could you better live for yourself and not others?

✔ What do you have that you are grateful for?

✔ How accepting of needed changes are you?

✔ How reliable are you?

✔ Describe what taking care of yourself means?

✔ What makes you laugh and live in the moment?

...and more Growth!

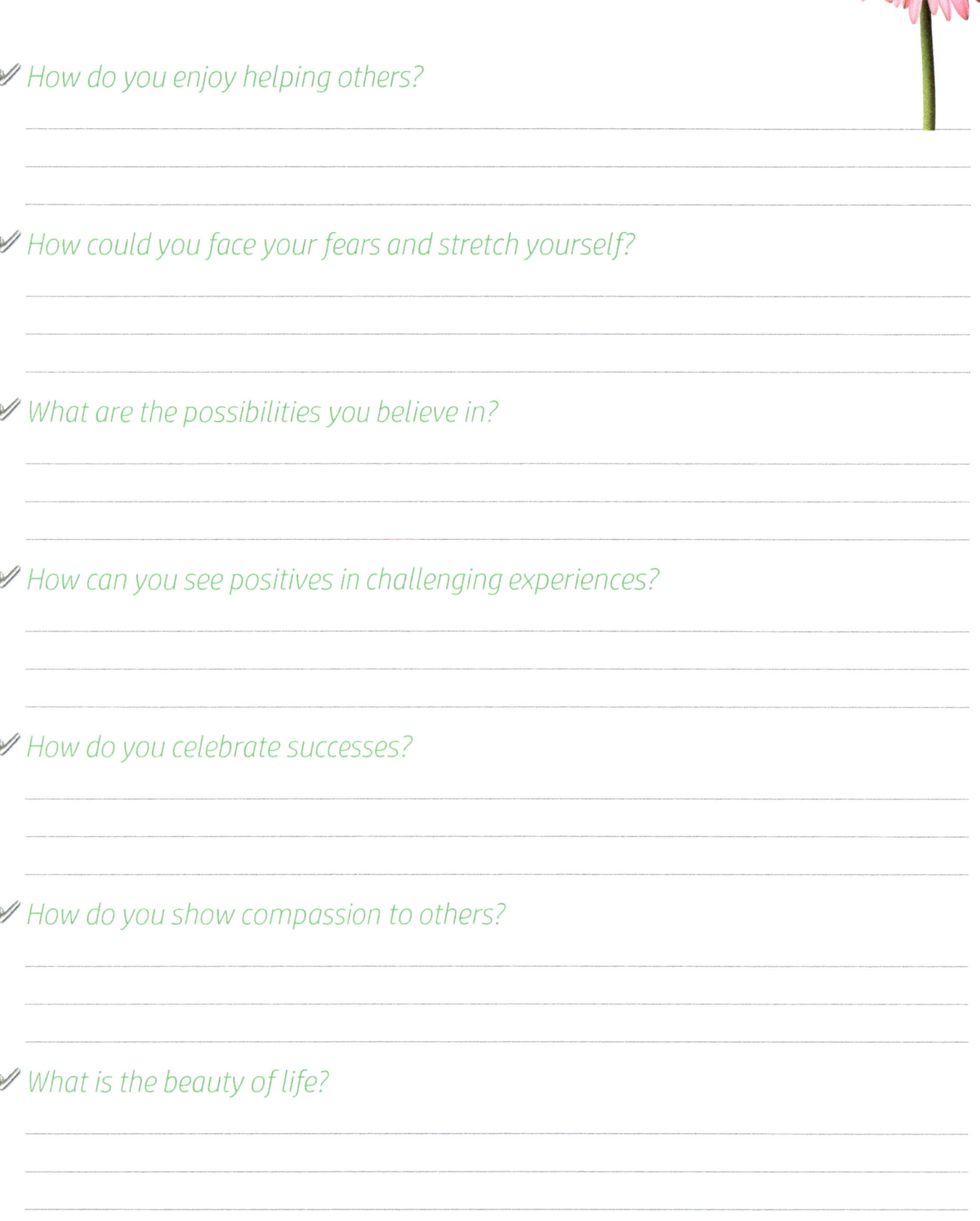

✔ *How do you enjoy helping others?*

✔ *How could you face your fears and stretch yourself?*

✔ *What are the possibilities you believe in?*

✔ *How can you see positives in challenging experiences?*

✔ *How do you celebrate successes?*

✔ *How do you show compassion to others?*

✔ *What is the beauty of life?*

How your life might be affected by not having Promise

- Not living your purpose
- Not living optimally
- Lack of believability and integrity
- Lack of respect from others
- Not being true to self
- Not living your dreams
- Frustrations
- No feeling of future possibilities
- Disconnect from others
- Nothing to look forward to

Some key words describing the opposite of Promise

bias	discrimination	indifference	distrust	betrayal
pretense	refusal	hesitancy	prejudice	refraction
denial	infidelity	deceit	hypocrisy	extremism
veto	disengagement	lie	rejection	disloyalty
treachery	falsehood	disagreement	bigotry	severance

My feelings about not having Promise…

_____
_____
_____
_____
_____
_____
_____
_____
_____

Words Are Valuable and Meaningful

PROMISE DEFINITIONS
- Commitment from one person to another
- Reason for feeling hopeful about the future
- Potential for achievement of excellence
- Cause for hope, expectation or assurance

Highlight the words that express the meaning of Promise to you.

conviction	commitment	endurance
demand	accordance	permission
standing	guarantee	arrangement
aspiration	contract	warranty
affection	optimism	compact
candor	acquiescence	validation
philanthropy	expectation	negotiation
avowal	insurance	achievement
sanction	corroboration	sensibility
bargain	honesty	promissory
oath	integrity	confirmation
acceptance	objectivity	word
recognition	humanity	generosity
concord	agreement	vow
significance	proclamation	affirmation
ambition	capitulation	undertaking
reliance	pact	endorsement
statement	legitimacy	swear
command	approval	obligation
surety	encouragement	assurance
declaration	covenant	hope
anticipation	settlement	dedication
earnest	attestation	requirement
pledge	reassurance	security
buoyancy	receptivity	certification

*Now go back and choose the five **most meaningful** words to describe Promise attributes you would like to have on your Pearl Strand and circle the butterfly beside them.*

78

*Describe each chosen Promise attribute you want on your
Pearl Strand, and why they are necessary
for your personal growth and well-being.
Then rate them 1-5 in order of importance to you.*

☐ _____

_____

_____

_____

☐ _____

_____

_____

_____

☐ _____

_____

_____

_____

☐ _____

_____

_____

_____

☐ _____

_____

_____

_____

Layering My Promise Pearl

What do I need?

Why do I want this?

When can I get started?

Layering My Promise Pearl

Where can I get what I need?

How can I get what I need?

Who can help me?

Defining Your Promise Value

Promise Attribute	If you have the attribute, how and when did you receive it?
	What were the influences that helped you?

Promise Attribute	If you have the attribute, how and when did you receive it?
	What were the influences that helped you?

Promise Attribute	If you have the attribute, how and when did you receive it?
	What were the influences that helped you?

Promise Attribute	If you have the attribute, how and when did you receive it?
	What were the influences that helped you?

Promise Attribute	If you have the attribute, how and when did you receive it?
	What were the influences that helped you?

Growing and Enhancing Your Promise Values

Want Value ⊙ Enhance Value ⊙ *Circle beside...* *whether you want* *to add the attribute* *to your life,* *Or* *Want to grow more* *attributes of the* *value that you have.*	*What is needed to string this pearl or add to its luster?* *How can you create or maintain the knot of this pearl?*
Want Value ⊙ Enhance Value ⊙ *Circle beside...* *whether you want* *to add the attribute* *to your life,* *Or* *Want to grow more* *attributes of the* *value that you have.*	*What is needed to string this pearl or add to its luster?* *How can you create or maintain the knot of this pearl?*
Want Value ⊙ Enhance Value ⊙ *Circle beside...* *whether you want* *to add the attribute* *to your life,* *Or* *Want to grow more* *attributes of the* *value that you have.*	*What is needed to string this pearl or add to its luster?* *How can you create or maintain the knot of this pearl?*
Want Value ⊙ Enhance Value ⊙ *Circle beside...* *whether you want* *to add the attribute* *to your life,* *Or* *Want to grow more* *attributes of the* *value that you have.*	*What is needed to string this pearl or add to its luster?* *How can you create or maintain the knot of this pearl?*
Want Value ⊙ Enhance Value ⊙ *Circle beside...* *whether you want* *to add the attribute* *to your life,* *Or* *Want to grow more* *attributes of the* *value that you have.*	*What is needed to string this pearl or add to its luster?* *How can you create or maintain the knot of this pearl?*

Making It Happen!

I am doing the work to live my Promise.

Task	How it will help me.	Start Date	Complete Date – C Or Ongoing – O
			C / O _____
			C / O _____
			C / O _____
			C / O _____
			C / O _____
			C / O _____
			C / O _____
			C / O _____
			C / O _____
			C / O _____
			C / O _____
			C / O _____
			C / O _____
			C / O _____
			C / O _____
			C / O _____
			C / O _____
			C / O _____

Task	How it will help me.	Start Date	Complete Date – C Or Ongoing - O

The Pearls of Wisdom in My Jewelry Box

My Promise Pearl Commitment

I will use the attributes that I have determined to be essential for becoming the person I aspire to be by…

_____

_____

_____

_____

and, furthermore I commit to maintaining the cycle of wisdom by sharing my knowledge with others by…

_____

_____

_____

_____

Power

"Power based on love is a thousand times more effective than one derived from fear of punishment."
~ *Mahatma Gandhi*

With Power you have the ability and consent to influence the outcome of events. You are the deciding factor and with that Power comes the responsibility to make decisions wisely, with much contemplation as to the consequences of your decision. More importantly, it is imperative that you do not abuse the privilege.

Power can also be recognized as your abilities and talents. You have insight to see things as opportunities and not problems. You are open to suggestions and ask for assistance as needed to achieve the best outcome.

You are in control of your thoughts, emotions, attitudes, and actions. You must be honest with yourself and others to maintain your integrity. Powerful people must be believable. Your leadership abilities inspire others to be their best and to have confidence to face their fears because they have witnessed your same self-determination. When there is something that needs to be done in your wheelhouse; you are the person they look to for assurance.

Life for you is viewed in successes, and you possess the courage needed to design the life you want to live. You demand and set high standards within yourself. You have the Power for choosing or losing those in your life who mirror your expectations.

If you are Powerful, you know your path and how to navigate through the journey. Likewise, you have the humility to acknowledge your mistakes and parlay them into learning and growth opportunities. You make no excuses for what you want and are truly willing to put in the work needed to make it come to fruition. Prioritizing tasks is seen as the best usage of your valuable resource of time.

How can you find your Power?

- Determining how you can help others
- Creating a plan to move vision into success
- Honesty and integrity in your actions
- Confidence in guiding others
- Ability to inspire yourself and others
- Commitment to see a task to completion

Potential challenges…

- Misuse of your authority
- Disconnection from others
- Lack of empathy
- Inability to accept differing perspectives and input

Benefits to you…

- Respect for yourself and others
- Organizational skills
- Self-assuredness
- Communication skills
- Accountability

"Power consists in one's capacity to link his will with the purpose of others, to lead by reason and a gift of cooperation."
~ *Woodrow Wilson*

Wise Power Words

What are the meanings of these proverbs to you?

"Power is strengthened by union."
~ LATIN

"He who strives to do, does more than he who has the power."
~ SPANISH

"The word of a powerful man is the truth."
~ BAMBARA

"Sincerity gives wings to power."
~ LATIN

"It is not in the pilot's power to prevent the wind from blowing."
~ SPANISH

"*Power acquired by guilt, is never used for a good purpose.*"
~ LATIN

"*He who is afraid of a thing gives it power over him.*"
~ SPANISH

"*A powerful man has big ears.*"
~ JAPANESE

"*Strong souls have willpower, weak ones only desires.*"
~ CHINESE

"*Honorable is the person who is aware of his power, yet refrains from inflicting bad things on others.*"
~ EGYPTIAN

"Listening well is just as powerful as talking well,
and is also as essential to true conversation."
~ CHINESE

"Take care when you speak in judgement, words are powerful weapons."
~ HOPI

"Though pepper is a tiny thing, its taste is mighty powerful."
~ ARABIC

"There are two powers to contend with,
those with a lot and those with nothing."
~ SICILIAN

"Wisdom is what makes a poor man a king, a weak person powerful,
a good generation of a bad one, a foolish man reasonable."
~ IRISH

Some questions and thoughts about your Power to consider...

✔ *How do you handle an opinion different from yours?*

✔ *What are the leadership skills you possess?*

✔ *What would it take to forgive someone when they hurt you?*

✔ *How can you mediate disputes?*

✔ *How can you rise above your fears?*

✔ *How do you show yourself to be believable?*

✔ *How persistent are you when you want to accomplish a task?*

...Tea and Thoughts...

✔ *How do you perceive asking for help?*

✔ *How flexible are you?*

✔ *How do you react when you make a mistake?*

✔ *How do you handle to-do lists?*

✔ *How do you share what you know?*

✔ *When do you doubt your decision-making abilities?*

✔ *How well do you accept compliments?*

...and More Growth!

✔ *In what ways are you prudent?*

✔ *How do you show self-control?*

✔ *How do you connect with others?*

✔ *How do you bring energy into situations?*

✔ *How do you show kindness?*

✔ *How comfortable are with taking the lead as needed?*

✔ *How do you manage your time?*

How your life might be affected by not using your Power

- ✓ Feeling chaotic
- ✓ Unable to forgive self and others
- ✓ Not feeling connected with a group
- ✓ Feeling you have no rights
- ✓ Inability to see things from different sides
- ✓ Unhealthy relationships
- ✓ Poor self-care
- ✓ Lack of coping skills
- ✓ Lack of integrity with others
- ✓ Inability to stand up for beliefs
- ✓ Poor self-control
- ✓ Not feeling driven

Some key words describing the opposite of Power

inability	impairment	sluggishness	incompetence	stiffness
inflexibility	surrender	condescension	laziness	inaptitude
negativity	incapacity	inadequacy	frailty	disdain
obstinacy	vulnerability	weakness	Insufficiency	snobbery
arrogance	inferiority	rigidity	paralysis	stubbornness

My feelings about not recognizing my Power…

_____
_____
_____
_____
_____
_____
_____

Words Are Valuable and Meaningful

POWER DEFINITIONS
- control or influence
- qualities needed to do something or get something done
- physical or mechanical strength
- authority or persuasive abilities

Highlight the words that express the meaning of Power to you.

determination	effectiveness	bravery
existence	flair	competence
impulse	propulsion	entrustment
dynamism	clout	character
inner force	hunger	adeptness
action	inventiveness	force
capability	efficacy	dignity
buoyancy	magnetism	insight
mission	impelling force	effervescence
diligence	expertise	charge
opportunity	amplitude	mandate
energy	flexibility	flame
qualification	fervency	obligation
birthright	fortitude	authority
perseverance	intelligence	stamina
fire	direction	finesse
potency	mastery	boldness
ardency	versatility	intensity
steam	inertia	drive
capability	privilege	dynamism
push	audacity	influence
genius	momentum	courage
determination	endurance	adaptability
personage	responsibility	heartiness
fuel	stalwartness	domination

*Now go back and choose the five **most meaningful** words to describe Power attributes you would like to have on your Pearl Strand and circle the butterfly beside them.*

*Describe each chosen Power attribute you want on your
Pearl Strand, and why they are necessary
for your personal growth and well-being.
Then rate them 1-5 in order of importance to you.*

☐ _____

_____
_____
_____

☐ _____

_____
_____
_____

☐ _____

_____
_____
_____

☐ _____

_____
_____
_____

☐ _____

_____
_____
_____

Layering My Power Pearl

What do I need?

Why do I want this?

When can I get started?

Layering My Power Pearl

Where can I get what I need?

How can I get what I need?

Who can help me?

Defining Your Power Value

Power Attribute	If you have the attribute, how and when did you receive it?
	What were the influences that helped you?

Power Attribute	If you have the attribute, how and when did you receive it?
	What were the influences that helped you?

Power Attribute	If you have the attribute, how and when did you receive it?
	What were the influences that helped you?

Power Attribute	If you have the attribute, how and when did you receive it?
	What were the influences that helped you?

Power Attribute	If you have the attribute, how and when did you receive it?
	What were the influences that helped you?

Growing and Enhancing Your Power Values

Want Value ⚪ **Enhance Value** ⚪ *Circle beside... whether you want to add the attribute to your life, Or Want to grow more attributes of the value that you have.*	*What is needed to string this pearl or add to its luster?* _____ _____ _____ *How can you create or maintain the knot of this pearl?* _____ _____ _____
Want Value ⚪ **Enhance Value** ⚪ *Circle beside... whether you want to add the attribute to your life, Or Want to grow more attributes of the value that you have.*	*What is needed to string this pearl or add to its luster?* _____ _____ _____ *How can you create or maintain the knot of this pearl?* _____ _____ _____
Want Value ⚪ **Enhance Value** ⚪ *Circle beside... whether you want to add the attribute to your life, Or Want to grow more attributes of the value that you have.*	*What is needed to string this pearl or add to its luster?* _____ _____ _____ *How can you create or maintain the knot of this pearl?* _____ _____ _____
Want Value ⚪ **Enhance Value** ⚪ *Circle beside... whether you want to add the attribute to your life, Or Want to grow more attributes of the value that you have.*	*What is needed to string this pearl or add to its luster?* _____ _____ _____ *How can you create or maintain the knot of this pearl?* _____ _____ _____
Want Value ⚪ **Enhance Value** ⚪ *Circle beside... whether you want to add the attribute to your life, Or Want to grow more attributes of the value that you have.*	*What is needed to string this pearl or add to its luster?* _____ _____ _____ *How can you create or maintain the knot of this pearl?* _____ _____ _____

Making It Happen!

I am doing the work to Recognize my Power.

Task	How it will help me.	Start Date	Complete Date - C Or Ongoing - O
			C ____ O ____
			C ____ O ____
			C ____ O ____
			C ____ O ____
			C ____ O ____
			C ____ O ____
			C ____ O ____
			C ____ O ____
			C ____ O ____
			C ____ O ____
			C ____ O ____
			C ____ O ____
			C ____ O ____
			C ____ O ____
			C ____ O ____
			C ____ O ____
			C ____ O ____

Task	How it will help me.	Start Date	Complete Date - C / Or / Ongoing - O

The Pearls of Wisdom in My Jewelry Box

My Power Pearl Commitment

I will use the attributes that I have determined to be essential for becoming the person I aspire to be by…

_____
_____
_____
_____

and, furthermore I commit to maintaining the cycle of wisdom by sharing my knowledge with others by…

_____
_____
_____
_____
_____

Peace

*"I do not want the peace that passeth understanding,
I want the understanding that bringeth peace."*
~ Helen Keller

There may certainly be physical conflicts and inequalities that require intervention to diffuse real and potential dangers. However, the reality is more often that the disquiet that is felt by a perception of the mind. Conflicts are invited into the thought process. As a situation presents, there is a determination made that something must be done to correct it.

The best arsenal for Peace is to equip yourself with tools needed to return to a calm and restful state of mind. Simply living can feel as if you are continually barraged with influencers that are determined to keep you anxious and unable to fully enjoy life.

Begin by evicting the tenants of your mind that are not paying rent to be there and are destroying the space. Kick them out of your thoughts so you can begin the remodeling. There will always be stressors coming at you, but being able and willing to abandon that which seeks to hold you down gives you buoyancy and resilience.

Peace is not a guaranteed constant even when you are doing everything you can to avoid letting in negative thoughts. Remember that you are charged and in control of how you react to the stressor. Sometimes you just have to let it go. It is not always necessary to win.

The best defense is to preliminarily create battle plans to neutralize the offending negative with a positive response such as relaxation, meditation, and comforting measures.

How can you find Peace?

- Understand what you want your life to be
- Recognize what is not working for you
- Make needed changes
- Connect with yourself and others
- Be in the moment, not dwelling on the past
- Set emotional boundaries and stick to them

Potential challenges...

- Disorganized environment
- Unrelieved stress
- Inability to let go.
- Criticizing yourself and others

Benefits to you...

- Your life feels balanced
- Feeling of satisfaction
- Seeing solutions in problems
- Becoming a part of your personal mission
- Self-acceptance

"Peace cannot be kept by force; it can only be achieved by understanding."
~Albert Einstein

Wise Peace Words

What are the meanings of these proverbs to you?

"A harvest of peace is produced from a seed of contentment."
~ AMERICAN

"Peace is costly but worth the expense."
~ AFRICAN

"Better a lean peace than a fat victory."
~ GERMAN

"Peace gains a value from discord."
~ LATIN

"Tell not all you know, nor judge of all you see, if you would live in peace."
~ SPANISH

"Peace feeds, war wastes; peace breeds, war consumes."
~ DANISH

"Better to keep peace than make peace."
~ DUTCH

"Peace is the well from which the stream of joy runs."
~ GAELIC

"To touch the earth is to have harmony with nature."
~ SIOUX

"Peace and harmony are great treasures."
~ RUSSIAN

"After the storm comes calm."
~ DUTCH

"Vows made in storm are forgotten in calm."
~ ENGLISH

"Don't think there are no crocodiles because the water's calm."
~ AFRICAN

"A soft answer calms the wrath."
~SWEDISH

"Wisdom and serenity should not unduly weigh down a person."
~ KASHMIRI

Some questions and thoughts about your Peace to consider...

- ✔ How is your health?

- ✔ When do you feel stressed?

- ✔ How comfortable are you with being quiet?

- ✔ When does your life feel as if it is in turmoil?

- ✔ How do you handle conflict?

- ✔ Describe past experiences that are nagging at you?

- ✔ What are your best memories?

...Tea and Thoughts...

✔ When do you engage in negative self-talk?
___

✔ How do you react to rumors and gossip?
___

✔ How is your sleep?
___

✔ How are your relationships with others?
___

✔ How do you rise above negative comments?
___

✔ How can you accept things for what they are?
___

✔ How do you handle emotional situations?
___

...and More Growth!

✔ *How comfortable are you with yourself?*
___

✔ *What are your spiritual beliefs?*
___

✔ *How do you relax?*
___

✔ *How does your environment and mind become cluttered or cleared?*
___

✔ *When do you disconnect from technology?*
___

✔ *How important is your opinion?*
___

✔ *How does conflict make you feel?*
___

How your life might be affected by not finding your Peace

- ✓ Increased worry
- ✓ Criticism of self and others
- ✓ Can't appreciate the good in life
- ✓ Negative preoccupation with the past
- ✓ Stress-related symptoms
- ✓ Disconnection with inner comfort
- ✓ Inability to let go and heal
- ✓ Missed opportunities
- ✓ Inability to talk through conflicts
- ✓ Poor mental focus
- ✓ Decreased happiness

Some key words describing the opposite of Peace

conflict	agitation	confrontation	antagonism	loathing
hostility	animosity	scorn	grievance	contention
opposition	despair	disagreement	commotion	aversion
rivalry	anxiety	antipathy	fighting	venom
tension	repulsion	uncertainty	chaos	tension

My thoughts about not feeling at Peace…

_____
_____
_____
_____
_____
_____
_____

Words Are Valuable and Meaningful

PEACE DEFINITIONS
- Mind calm and at ease
- Agreement reached after conflict
- Freedom from disturbance
- State of quietness and repose

Highlight the words that express the meaning of Peace to you.

ease	forgiveness	civil
mercy	composure	goodwill
cohesion	affinity	recovered
recreation	reconciliation	nirvana
fellowship	exhaling	kinship
rejoiced	mediation	agreement
accord	comfort	softness
rest	self-composure	leisure
alliance	happiness	retirement
oneness	security	compatibility
relaxation	symbiosis	symbiosis
contentment	amity	moratorium
joy	patience	symphony
quiet	restoration	bliss
benevolence	calm	consensus
serenity	silence	poise
order	healing	sedateness
cooperation	solidarity	tranquility
reassured	blessedness	assent
sedateness	pleasure	repose
breathing	rapport	stillness
pacification	respite	amicability
stabilized	cooperation	justice
heartsease	unity	organization
successful	soothed	confident

*Now go back and choose the five **most meaningful** words to describe Peace attributes you would like to have on your Pearl Strand and circle the butterfly beside them.*

*Describe each chosen Peace attribute you want on your
Pearl Strand, and why they are necessary
for your personal growth and well-being.
Then rate them 1-5 in order of importance to you.*

Layering My Peace Pearl

What do I need?

Why do I want this?

When can I get started?

Layering My Peace Pearl

Where can I get what I need?

How can I get what I need?

Who can help me?

Defining Your Peace Value

Peace Attribute	If you have the attribute, how and when did you receive it?
	What were the influences that helped you?

Peace Attribute	If you have the attribute, how and when did you receive it?
	What were the influences that helped you?

Peace Attribute	If you have the attribute, how and when did you receive it?
	What were the influences that helped you?

Peace Attribute	If you have the attribute, how and when did you receive it?
	What were the influences that helped you?

Peace Attribute	If you have the attribute, how and when did you receive it?
	What were the influences that helped you?

Growing and Enhancing Your Peace Values

Want Value ○ Enhance Value ○ *Circle beside... whether you want to add the attribute to your life, Or Want to grow more attributes of the value that you have.*	What is needed to string this pearl or add to its luster? _____ _____ How can you create or maintain the knot of this pearl? _____ _____ _____
Want Value ○ Enhance Value ○ *Circle beside... whether you want to add the attribute to your life, Or Want to grow more attributes of the value that you have.*	What is needed to string this pearl or add to its luster? _____ _____ How can you create or maintain the knot of this pearl? _____ _____ _____
Want Value ○ Enhance Value ○ *Circle beside... whether you want to add the attribute to your life, Or Want to grow more attributes of the value that you have.*	What is needed to string this pearl or add to its luster? _____ _____ How can you create or maintain the knot of this pearl? _____ _____ _____
Want Value ○ Enhance Value ○ *Circle beside... whether you want to add the attribute to your life, Or Want to grow more attributes of the value that you have.*	What is needed to string this pearl or add to its luster? _____ _____ How can you create or maintain the knot of this pearl? _____ _____ _____
Want Value ○ Enhance Value ○ *Circle beside... whether you want to add the attribute to your life, Or Want to grow more attributes of the value that you have.*	What is needed to string this pearl or add to its luster? _____ _____ How can you create or maintain the knot of this pearl? _____ _____ _____

Making It Happen!

I am doing the work to live my Peace.

Task	How it will help me.	Start Date	Complete Date – C Or Ongoing – O

Task	How it will help me.	Start Date	Complete Date – C Or Ongoing - O
			C O
			C O
			C O
			C O
			C O
			C O
			C O
			C O
			C O
			C O
			C O
			C O
			C O
			C O
			C O
			C O
			C O
			C O
			C O
			C O
			C O
			C O
			C O
			C O
			C O

The Pearls of Wisdom in My Jewelry Box

My Peace Pearl Commitment

I will use the attributes that I have determined to be essential for becoming the person I aspire to be by...

_____

_____

_____

_____

and, furthermore I commit to maintaining the cycle of wisdom by sharing my knowledge with others by...

_____

_____

_____

_____

Path

"Only those who will risk going too far can possibly find out how far we can go."

~ T. S. Eliot

Your Life Path is uniquely yours. Sometimes you may find the direction is not as what you thought it should be. Part of getting on – and staying – on the path is remaining open to changes. There may be many side trips of needed learning experiences before you converge back on the main path. When you know your Life Path, you are compelled to move forward at all costs and feel a sense of accomplishment with each leg of the journey.

Knowing the direction helps avoid unnecessary and non-productive efforts. Without insight you can become frustrated and lost. With knowledge, experience and intuition, some of the anxiety is taken out of the journey. Decision-making and planning become easier and help you avoid wasting valuable and often limited resources such as time and money.

You must be flexible to navigate the unpredictable twists and curves; they are there to teach you valuable lessons. Your interests remain piqued and they are often small exercises in preparation for something larger. If you allow changes to your routine, the newness creates a discomfort that forces you to challenge and extend yourself outside your comfort zone. You will have a different visual perspective.

Challenges are only roadblocks if you allow yourself to see them as such. Watch your step and don't take opportunities for granted. They may not reappear when you want them.

If you do not know what your Life Path is yet, you may help discover it by listening to those inner voices, telling you what is important to you, and what you need to do to make your personal difference. As always, try new things to find what you enjoy, and why you feel a desire to do more.

How can you begin your Life Path?

- Listen to your inner voice
- Believe in yourself as successful
- Let go of the status quo
- Evaluate what you are doing or not doing
- Use past experiences to help you
- Pursue your interests

Potential challenges…

- Everyday life occurrences
- Excessive and rigid practices
- Resisting what you know is needed
- Allowing distractions to interrupt progress

Benefits to you…

- You get out of your own way
- Excitement about your life journey
- Adaptability to change
- Ability to create solutions
- Stronger connections with yourself and others

"It isn't where you come from; it's where you're going that counts."

~ Ella Fitzgerald

Wise Life Path Words

What are the meanings of these proverbs to you?

"I dreamed a thousand new paths...I woke and walked my old one."
~ CHINESE

"A well-beaten path does not always make the right road."
~ LATIN

"Every path has its puddle."
~ ENGLISH

"If you don't know where you are going, any path will take you there."
~ SIOUX

"Don't allow the grass to grow on the path of friendship."
~ AMERICAN

"It is often better to go by a circuitous than by a direct path."
~ LATIN

"There are many paths to the top of the mountain; but the view is always the same."
~ CHINESE

"The path is made by walking."
~ AFRICAN

"There are a thousand paths to every wrong."
~ POLISH

"Who does not know the path should ask."
~ NILOTIC

"On an unknown path every foot is slow."
~ AMERICAN

"Do not follow the path. Go where there is no path to begin the trail."
~ AFRICAN

"The obstacle is the path."
~ ZEN

"Misfortunes do not flourish on one path, they grow everywhere."
~ PAWNEE

"The daily path never ends."
~ AFRICAN

Some questions and thoughts about your Life Path to consider...

✔ How do you plan for travel?

✔ How organized are you?

✔ What do you do when you encounter obstacles?

✔ How do you decide the best way to proceed when offered choices?

✔ What are you waiting for?

✔ When do you procrastinate to avoid doing things?

✔ How well can you see beyond what is in front of you?

...Tea and Thoughts...

✔ *What motivates you to take chances?*

✔ *At what pace do you think your life is moving?*

✔ *What are your intuitive signs telling you?*

✔ *How are you enjoying life?*

✔ *What are the distractions that need to be removed?*

✔ *What are the recurring situations that keep drawing you to them?*

✔ *How open are you to trying new ways of doing things?*

...and More Growth!

✔ How do you set goals?
_____
_____
_____

✔ How do you lighten the mood when things are too serious?
_____
_____
_____

✔ How could you simplify your life?
_____
_____
_____

✔ Who or what inspires you?
_____
_____
_____

✔ When is it necessary to learn new things?
_____
_____
_____

✔ How flexible are you with changes in plans?
_____
_____
_____

✔ When are risks necessary?
_____
_____
_____

How your life might be affected without navigating your Life Path

- Feeling that something is missing from your life
- Often feeling ill
- Sense that nothing is going right
- Excessive in behaviors
- Always searching for something more
- Avoidance of uncomfortable situations
- Feeling a need to move obstacles out of your life
- Not living up to your potential
- Complaining a lot
- Feeling like you're in a rut

Some key words describing the opposite of Path

detour	circumvention	blockage	deflection	idleness
inactivity	wrong way	inertia	immobility	motionlessness
substitute	deviation	departure	closure	digression
bypass	lock	exit	stillness	Alternate
abstention	stagnation	diversion	inaction	dormancy

My feelings about not understanding my Path in life...

_____
_____
_____
_____
_____
_____
_____
_____
_____

Words Are Valuable and Meaningful

PATH DEFINITIONS
- A course for conducting life
- Route for moving or traveling
- Direction a person or object is moving

Highlight the words that express the meaning of a Path to you.

process	route	crossing
door	access	journey
road	step	transit
flow	egress	aim
tour	marathon	footpath
bearing	plot	trace
junket	tactic	channel
way forward	bridge	progress
map	locomotion	wanderlust
trajectory	range	transition
freeway	heading	way of life
escape	trail	conveyance
gateway	stretch	plan
travel	voyage	technique
way out	course	mode
conduit	excursion	means
stroll	passage	trip
corridor	highway	race
trek	expedition	orientation
escapade	direction	walk
transport	strategy	navigation
climb	promenade	track
drive	loop	movement
hike	march	approach
circuit	cycle	distance

*Now go back and choose the five **most meaningful** words to describe Life Path attributes you would like to have on your Pearl Strand and circle the butterfly beside them.*

132

Describe each chosen Life Path attribute you want on your Pearl Strand, and why they are necessary for your personal growth and well-being. Then rate them 1-5 in order of importance to you.

☐ _____

_____
_____
_____

☐ _____

_____
_____
_____

☐ _____

_____
_____
_____

☐ _____

_____
_____
_____

☐ _____

_____
_____
_____

Layering My Life Path Pearl

What do I need?

Why do I want this?

When can I get started?

Layering My Life Path Pearl

Where can I get what I need?

How can I get what I need?

Who can help me?

Defining Your Life Path Value

Life Path Attribute	If you have the attribute, how and when did you receive it?
	What were the influences that helped you?

Life Path Attribute	If you have the attribute, how and when did you receive it?
	What were the influences that helped you?

Life Path Attribute	If you have the attribute, how and when did you receive it?
	What were the influences that helped you?

Life Path Attribute	If you have the attribute, how and when did you receive it?
	What were the influences that helped you?

Life Path Attribute	If you have the attribute, how and when did you receive it?
	What were the influences that helped you?

Growing and Enhancing Your Life Path Values

Want Value ⚪ **Enhance Value** ⚪ *Circle beside... whether you want to add the attribute to your life, Or Want to grow more attributes of the value that you have.*	*What is needed to string this pearl or add to its luster?* _____ _____ *How can you create or maintain the knot of this pearl?* _____ _____ _____
Want Value ⚪ **Enhance Value** ⚪ *Circle beside... whether you want to add the attribute to your life, Or Want to grow more attributes of the value that you have.*	*What is needed to string this pearl or add to its luster?* _____ _____ *How can you create or maintain the knot of this pearl?* _____ _____ _____
Want Value ⚪ **Enhance Value** ⚪ *Circle beside... whether you want to add the attribute to your life, Or Want to grow more attributes of the value that you have.*	*What is needed to string this pearl or add to its luster?* _____ _____ *How can you create or maintain the knot of this pearl?* _____ _____ _____
Want Value ⚪ **Enhance Value** ⚪ *Circle beside... whether you want to add the attribute to your life, Or Want to grow more attributes of the value that you have.*	*What is needed to string this pearl or add to its luster?* _____ _____ *How can you create or maintain the knot of this pearl?* _____ _____ _____
Want Value ⚪ **Enhance Value** ⚪ *Circle beside... whether you want to add the attribute to your life, Or Want to grow more attributes of the value that you have.*	*What is needed to string this pearl or add to its luster?* _____ _____ *How can you create or maintain the knot of this pearl?* _____ _____ _____

Making It Happen!

I am doing the work to follow my Life Path.

Task	How it will help me.	Start Date	Complete Date – C Or Ongoing - O

Task	How it will help me.	Start Date	Complete Date C Or Ongoing - O
			C / O

The Pearls of Wisdom in My Jewelry Box

My Life Path Pearl Commitment

I will use the attributes that I have determined to be essential for becoming the person I aspire to be by…

_____

_____

_____

_____

and, furthermore I commit to maintaining the cycle of wisdom by sharing my knowledge with others by…

_____

_____

_____

_____

Writing Your Personal Mission Statement

You have defined the seven core values that express how you want to live and how you are going to acquire, grow, and enhance them. It is time now to pull all those pieces of information together.

Your Personal Mission Statement is your introduction to others – whether they already know you or not – as to who you are and what you stand for. It is your personal billboard.

Other people will know the wisdom you possess and aspire to include in your life. They will see how you will use that knowledge, not only to become your best but also committed to share with others so that they too may incorporate whatever is useful for them to enhance their lives.

Your Personal Mission Statement clearly and concisely defines your guiding principles, and your desire for self-fulfillment. It demonstrates what you believe you have been called upon to do and the choices you have made that align with the values you have outlined.

The statements you proclaim will provide the legacy that will survive long after you are gone, as to how you personally impacted others by your existence.

All of our lives touch others in varying ways and those contacts grow exponentially. This spread of experiences reinforces the value each of us possesses and the importance of living our best life.

A Personal Mission Statement is a living document not only in that it gives a snapshot of your commitments for daily living but also it grows as you grow.

This document should be revisited at least yearly, and more often if your needs change, to maintain its value to your life.

To complete this document, go back to the final worksheet for each of your values, and write a short sentence that states your intent. Then fill in the areas of the Mission Statement form when you are satisfied with the message content.

Place a copy of your Personal Mission Statement where you can see it daily as a reminder of your plans and how you will use opportunities for living it and sharing it.

Concise Value Statements

Purpose

_____
_____

Passion

_____
_____

Presents

_____
_____

Promise

_____
_____

Power

_____
_____

Peace

_____
_____

Path

_____
_____

My Personal Mission

_____

Date _____

My mission in life is to…
_____
_____
_____

I will achieve this mission by utilizing my identified Seven Pearls of Wisdom core values as follows:

- ⚪ *Presents*
  _____
  _____

- ⚪ *Purpose*
  _____
  _____

- ⚪ *Promise*
  _____
  _____

- ⚪ *Passion*
  _____
  _____

- ⚪ *Power*
  _____
  _____

- ⚪ *Peace*
  _____
  _____

- ⚪ *Path*
  _____
  _____

The Pearls I have defined will positively impact the lives of others by…
_____
_____

I commit to daily enhancing my Pearls and thereby optimizing my life by…
_____
_____
_____

For Those Very Special To Me

First, before anything else, I want to thank God for the wisdom and direction that has cleared my path onward, I could not have done it alone.

I am grateful for all the family members, friends, acquaintances, and group participants who have allowed me into their lives throughout my life, and career. You have all encouraged me to learn and share information and experiences, as we all grew stronger.

My daughter, Courtney, and grandchildren, Tavion and Valerie, I thank you for giving me love and smiles. You are such lovely and treasured gifts to my life.

Tom, you have provided me the love and support that you will never fully understand that has made this project possible.

Fern Mann, your editing and suggestions are greatly appreciated as well as the encouragement to keep writing.

Last, and certainly not least the team of Momosa Publishing, Hannah thank you for your editing, and Jennifer - your friendship and belief in my ideas came into my life at just the right time to help me pull this together and inspiration for me to continue moving forward.

About the Author

A nursing career of more than 25 years primarily in community health education has afforded me the opportunity to learn and share with those who invited me into their lives. My strongest belief has always been a need to listen for the wishes of individuals and to coach them through a self-paced walk of bringing those desires to fruition.

This series of Seven Pearls of Wisdom for Wellness Lifebooks has been a lifetime in the making as I have gathered the necessary knowledge to add to my personal Jewelry Box. Sometimes I thought I wanted to depart from my purpose and life path to do other things but I always found myself being drawn back to my personal mission. The departures I have discovered were merely opportunities for me to gain additional valuable information, and they put me back on my journey.

The purpose of the Seven Pearls of Wisdom for Wellness Lifebooks is so that we may each seed our own pearls and continually add the beautiful layers in preparation for harvesting our pearls so we may proudly wear them to remind ourselves and show others who we are and how we value our lives. A valuable pearl needs a strong and reliable shell to transform the seed of change by continually adding protective and beatifying layers. With *Seven Pearls of Wellness for Wisdom – Jewelry Box,* we grow, harvest and string those beautiful valuable pearls. The most wonderful thing is that we each have what is needed within us ready to begin the process for adding our pearls to those other gems we treasure. Pearls require preventive maintenance and sometimes repairs to keep their value.

Seven Pearls of Wisdom for Wellness – Jewelry Box stimulates those thoughts and self-questioning that helps us to access information about who we are, what we desire, and how we can become the people we aspire to be. Usually, we see change as a sacrifice or loss of who we are. We may feel who we are and what we believe are all wrong in comparison to others. The reality is that this is simply not true. Change is individual, and improvements upon ourselves are uniquely individual. Life is for enjoying and making changes is a way better enjoy and appreciate the time we are given and share with others. We create a scrapbook of memories to flip through and smile as we recall the experiences.

I have decided the next volume *Seven Pearls of Wisdom for Wellness – Living and Loving Life!* is necessary to remind us to remain joyful as we move along the journey of our lives and as we incorporate the values we define in this Seven Pearls of Wisdom for Wellness Lifebook to become our best selves.

*Contact me for information about other
Seven Pearls of Wisdom for Wellness lifebooks
in the series and companion products,
which support and enhance your discoveries.*

Lifebook Volume 2

Seven Pearls of Wisdom for Wellness

Living and Loving Life!

Focusing on ideas for rejuvenating yourself
with the joy, laughter, and energy you deserve,
to keep moving on your life journey

Lifebook Volume 3

Seven Pearls of Wisdom for Wellness

Telling My Story

Utilizing your health history and baseline information
sets a framework for determining
what you want and need
to optimally write your best life story.

Lifebook Volume 4

Seven Pearls of Wisdom for Wellness

What's Cooking?

Choosing a nutrition and movement program
that fits your wants, abilities, and needs
is important to being able to maximize the benefits
and maintain a lifestyle plan.

Add yourself to the mailing list for availability,
release, and ordering updates.
Group discounts and facilitation supports
are also available upon request.
info@sagesselife.com

Sage Life
Wisdom for Wellness